A MIDSUMMER NIGHT'S DREAM

by
William Shakespeare

Student Packet

Written by
Gloria Levine, M.A.

Contains masters for:

1	Prereading Activity
3	Vocabulary Activities
1	Study Guide
1	Critical Thinking Activity
2	Literary Analysis Activities
3	Writing Activities
1	Comprehension Activity
2	Language Study Activities
2	Comprehension Quizzes (two levels)
2	Unit Exams (two levels)

PLUS   Detailed Answer Key

Note

The text used to prepare this guide was the Bantam Classic softcover edited by David Bevington and with a foreword by Joseph Papp, ©1988.

Please note: Please assess the appropriateness of this book for the age level and maturity of your students prior to reading and discussing it with your class.

ISBN 1-56137-519-5

To order, contact your local school supply store, or—

Novel Units, Inc.
P.O. Box 97
Bulverde, TX 78163-0097

Web site: www.educyberstor.com

Shakespeare used many words that are now rare or obsolete—or mean something else. When he couldn't quite find the word to suit his meaning, he frequently made one up! It's not important to understand the meaning of every word or line that he wrote. What matters is that you enjoy his wonderful—and often playful—use of language.

Group activity: Before you read or view *A Midsummer Night's Dream,* take a look at the following list of words from the play. Brainstorm possible definitions and use each word or phrase in a sentence. Have fun writing imaginative sentences—and later comparing your definitions with the actual ones.

1. mewed (1.1. 71 = Act 1. scene 1. line 71)
2. waggish (1.1. 240)
3. lob (2.1.16)
4. quern (2.1. 36)
5. oxlips (2.1. 250)
6. reremice (2.2. 4)
7. beshrew (2.2. 60)
8. pat (3.1. 2)
9. parlous (3.1. 12)
10. eke (3.1. 90)
11. throstle (3.1. 122)
12. gleek (3.1. 141)
13. mortal grossness (3.1. 154)
14. peascod (3.1. 182)
15. rude mechanicals (3.2. 9)
16. o'er shoes (3.2. 48)
17. aby (3.2. 175)
18. recreant (3.2. 409)
19. Jack shall have Jill (3.2. 461)
20. dewlapped (4.1. 121)

Act I, Scene i

1. Who is Theseus? Why is he anxious for the rising of the new moon? What does he tell Philostrate to do?
2. Why is Egeus angry? Why has he come to see Theseus?
3. What are your impressions of Hermia? Whom does she love?
4. What alternatives does Theseus offer Hermia? In what tone do you imagine him presenting these alternatives?
5. How does Hermia change during her time alone with Lysander? Where do Lysander and Hermia agree to meet that night? Why?
6. What is the relationship between Hermia and Helena?
7. How does Helena betray the secret Hermia tells her? Why?
8. Why do you suppose Egeus prefers Demetrius to Lysander?
9. Paraphrase Hermia's speech, lines 150-155.

Prediction: Do you think that Hermia and Lysander will succeed in their plans for elopement?

Act I, Scene ii

1. What is the purpose of the meeting at Peter Quince's house?
2. Who is Nick Bottom? How does he make trouble at the meeting?
3. Briefly, what is the plot of *Pyramus and Thisbe?* Do you think this is an appropriate choice of entertainment at a wedding?
4. How are Pyramus and Thisbe like Hermia and Lysander?
5. What part will Bottom play?
6. How do the names of the tradesmen fit their occupations?
7. What part will Snug play? What is funny about his asking whether his lines will be written out?
8. When and where do the tradesmen plan to rehearse?
9. Cite evidence that Bottom is "talking through his hat" when he pretends to know that the play is "a very good piece of work." Which line tells you that he isn't really familiar with the play?

Prediction: Do you think the tradesmen will end up with a polished performance? Will Theseus and Hippolyta be pleased with it?

4

Act II, Scene i

1. By what other name is Puck known?

2. What does the fairy tell Puck at the beginning of this scene? What warning does he give her, in turn?

3. Why is Oberon angry with Titania? Why does he want the boy?

4. What sorts of tricks does Puck play on humans? Why? Can you think of some other tricks he might play—but doesn't mention?

5. Why is Titania jealous of Hippolyta? Of whom is Oberon jealous?

6. Who do Titania and Oberon blame for recent storms and floods? Who do you think is more to blame?

7. According to Oberon, how did the pansy become magical? Why does he tell Puck to fetch the flower?

8. Who races after Demetrius into the woods? How does he try to stop her?

9. Paraphrase Helena's speech, lines 238-244.

Prediction: Do you think Oberon's plan for the magic nectar will work?

Act II, Scene ii

1. What jobs does Titania send her fairies off to do?

2. Why do the fairies sing charms for Titania?

3. Why does Oberon pronounce a spell over Titania?

4. Why does Lysander move away from Hermia before they sleep?

5. On whose eyelids does Puck press the magic nectar? Why?

6. What happens when Helena wakens Lysander? What does she think of his flattery?

7. What has Hermia been dreaming about?

8. Why does Hermia run off at the end of the scene?

9. Paraphrase Lysander's speech, lines 141-150.

Prediction: With whom will Titania fall in love, thanks to the magic nectar?

Act III, Scene i

1. Why is Bottom worried about the ladies in the audience? What solution does he offer?

2. What problem worries Snout? What solution does Bottom come up with?

3. Why does Bottom propose looking in an almanac?

4. Why does Quince decide to have Starveling carry a thornbush?

5. How does Bottom propose that Snout make the part of the wall more realistic?

6. How does Puck play tricks on the actors in the wood?

7. How does Bottom react when he realizes that he has the head of an ass?

8. How does Titania react when she sees Bottom? What orders does she give her four tiny fairies?

9. Explain Bottom's comments to Cobweb, lines 177-179.

Prediction: Who will "win" Helena—Lysander or Demetrius?

Act III, Scene ii

1. How does Oberon learn that Titania is in love with Bottom? How does he feel about that?

2. How does Oberon realize that Puck has made a mistake and bewitched the wrong Athenian youth?

3. What does Hermia think has happened to Lysander? Why does she think so?

4. On whom does Oberon press the magical nectar now? Why?

5. How does Helena react when Demetrius declares his love? Why?

6. Why do Hermia and Helena argue?

7. Who challenges whom to a duel? Why?

8. What does Oberon order Puck to do to set things right on earth?

9. Paraphrase Puck's final speech in this scene.

Prediction: Will Oberon succeed in "setting things right" on earth and in the world of the fairies?

Act IV, Scene i

1. How is Titania showing her affection for Bottom at the beginning of this scene? Who else is present—unnoticed by her?

2. What sort of music and food does Bottom request?

3. How does Oberon get the little boy?

4. Why does Oberon return Titania to normal?

5. How do Theseus, Egeus and the others happen to find the four lovers? Why is Theseus surprised by their appearance?

6. What would Egeus like Theseus to do? What does Theseus do instead?

7. When they all awaken, how much do the lovers and Bottom remember about the previous night?

8. What does Bottom plan to have Peter Quince write? Why? How do you feel toward Bottom, now that he is back to "normal"? Do you pity him?

9. Paraphrase Theseus' comments to the lovers and to Egeus, lines 176-185.

Prediction: What have Bottom's fellow craftsmen been doing since he disappeared? Have they missed him?

Act IV, Scene ii

1. Why are the tradesmen upset? Why don't they just assign someone else the role of Pyramus?

2. What news does Snug bring? How does this make the tradesmen feel?

3. Why does Flute say that Bottom "hath...lost six-pence a day during his life"?

4. How do the tradesmen find out that their play has been put on the "preferred list"?

5. What does Bottom tell the others to do in preparation for the play?

6. Explain what Snug means by lines lines 15-18.

Prediction: Will the three marriages take place without a "hitch"?

Act V, Scene i

1. Who is married in this scene?

2. Why does Theseus choose *Pyramus and Thisbe* over the other shows he might watch?

3. How does Quince manage to make the Prologue to the play unintentionally funny?

4. How is Hippolyta's reaction to the players different from Theseus', at first?

5. Why does "Pyramus" (Bottom) curse the wall?

6. Why does "Moonshine" speak in prose instead of verse? What does he say?

7. How does the audience react as the suicides (of Pyramus and Thisbe) are being enacted?

8. What choices does Bottom give Theseus at the end of the play? What does Theseus choose?

9. Who enters as the newly-married couples go off to bed? What does Oberon give to each fairy? Why?

10. Explain the directions Oberon gives the fairies in lines 386-391.

11. What is Puck doing at the end as he describes the night? For what does he apologize?

Vocabulary List:

troth	livery	darkling	reremice
collied	condole	changeling	brakes
buskined	leviathan		

  I.   Fill in each blank with the appropriate vocabulary word from the list. The quotes are taken from Acts I and II.

1. "Examine...whether, if you yield not to your father's choice
You can endure the _____ of a nun."

2. "Or if there were a sympathy in choice
War, death, or sickness did lay siege to it
Making it...Brief as the lightning in the _____ night."

3. "That will ask some tears in the true performing of it...
I will move storms; I will _____ in some measure."

4. "...she as her attendant hath a lovely boy, stolen from an Indian king;
She never had so sweet a _____."

5. "Why art thou here...But that, forsooth, the bouncing Amazon,
Your _____ mistress ...To Theseus must be wedded."

6. "Fetch me this herb, and be thou here again
Ere the _____ can swim a league."

7. "I'll run from thee and hide me in the _____,
And leave thee to the mercy of wild beasts."

8. "Some war with _____ for their leathern wings
To make my small elves coats."

9. "One turf shall serve as pillow for us both;
One heart, one bed, two bosoms, and one _____ "

10. "O, wilt thou _____—leave me? Do not so."

II. Identify the speaker and the person addressed for each of the quotes.

<u>**Speaker**</u>   <u>**Person**</u> <u>**Addressed**</u>

1. _____   _____

2. _____   _____

3. _____   _____

4. _____   _____

5. _____   _____

6. _____   _____

7. _____   _____

8. _____   _____

9. _____   _____

10. _____   _____

III. Write each word on the list next to its correct definition.

_____	a. in the dark	_____	f. arouse pity
_____	b. whale, sea monster	_____	g. child exchanged for another by the fairies
_____	c. wearing half-boots	_____	h. faith
_____	d. clothes, habit	_____	i. thickets
_____	e. bats	_____	j. blackened

Vocabulary List:

incorporate	stealth	misprision	gleek
engilds	derision	welkin	patches
throstle	juvenal		

I. Fill in the blanks with the appropriate vocabulary word from Act III.

1. "Most radiant Pyramus,...Most brisky _____ and eke most lovely Jew"

2. "But I will not stir from this place, do what they can...
   The ouzel cock so black of hue...
   The _____ with his note so true."

3. "And yet, to say the truth, reason an love keep little company together
   nowadays...Nay, I can _____upon occasion."

4. "My mistress with a monster is in love...
   A crew of _____, rude mechanicals, ...
   Were met together to rehearse a play."

5. "What hast thou done?...Of thy _____ must perforce ensue
   Some true love turned, and not a false turned true."

6. "Fair Helena, who more _____the night
   Than all yon fiery oes and eyes of light."

7. "We...like two artificial gods
   Have with our needles created both one floweur...
   As if your hands, our sides, voices, and minds
   Had been _____."

8. "I evermore did love you...Did ever keep your counsels, never wronged you
   Save that, in love unto Demetrius,
   I told him of your _____unto this wood."

9. "Hie...overcast the night
   The starry _____cover thou anon
   With drooping fog."

10. "When they next awake, all this _____
    Shall seem a dream and fruitless vision."

II.   Identify the speaker and the audience for each of the quotes.

<u>**Speaker**</u>   **Person Addressed**

1.   _____   _____

2.   _____   _____

3.   _____   _____

4.   _____   _____

5.   _____   _____

6.   _____   _____

7.   _____   _____

8.   _____   _____

9.   _____   _____

10. _____   _____

III.   Match the words with their definitions.

a. mistake_____   f. sky_____

b. laughable business_____   g. youth_____

c. clowns, fools_____   h. scoff, jest_____

d. brightens with a golden light   i. songbird_____
    _____

                                        j. of one body_____

e. sneaking away_____

Vocabulary List:

masques	imbrue	patched	brands
gaud	hight	mend	pumps
moused	prodigious		

I. Fill in the blanks with the appropriate vocabulary word from Act IV or Act V.

1. "...my love to Hermia
Melted as the snow, seems to me now
As the remembrance of an idle _____."

2. "...man is but a _____ fool if he will offer to say what methought I had."

3. "Get your apparel together—new ribbons to your _____ "

4. "Come now, what _____ , what dances shall we have
To wear away this long age of three hours."

5. "This grisly beast, which Lion _____ by name."

6. "Well _____, Lion."

7. "Come, blade, my breast _____!"

8. "Now the wasted _____ do glow."

9. "Never mole, harelip, nor scar, nor mark _____....shall upon their children be."

10. "If you pardon, we will _____."

13

II. Identify the speaker and the audience for each of the quotes.

Speaker   **Person Addressed**

1. _____   _____

2. _____   _____

3. _____   _____

4. _____   _____

5. _____   _____

6. _____   _____

7. _____   _____

8. _____   _____

9. _____   _____

10. _____   _____

III. Match the words with their definitions.

a. logs_____   f. courtly entertainments

                                                     _____

b. is called_____   g. bloodstained_____

c. improve_____   h. trinket_____

d. monstrous_____   i. light shoes_____

e. shaken, torn, bitten   j. wearing a dress of many colors

 _____   _____

Directions: Graphics (drawings) can be used to help you think about and remember relationships between characters. Below is a list of characters in *A Midsummer Night's Dream*.

Theseus	Hermia	Peter Quince	Peaseblossom
Egeus	Helena	Nick Bottom	Cobweb
Lysander	Oberon	Francis Flute	Moth
Demetrius	Titania	Tom Snout	Mustardseed
Philostrate	Puck	Snug	Robin Starveling
Hippolyta			

The clusters below show relationships between various characters at the beginning of the play. Fill in the character names that you feel fit in each circle. (A few clue-labels have been provided.)

At the beginning of the play:

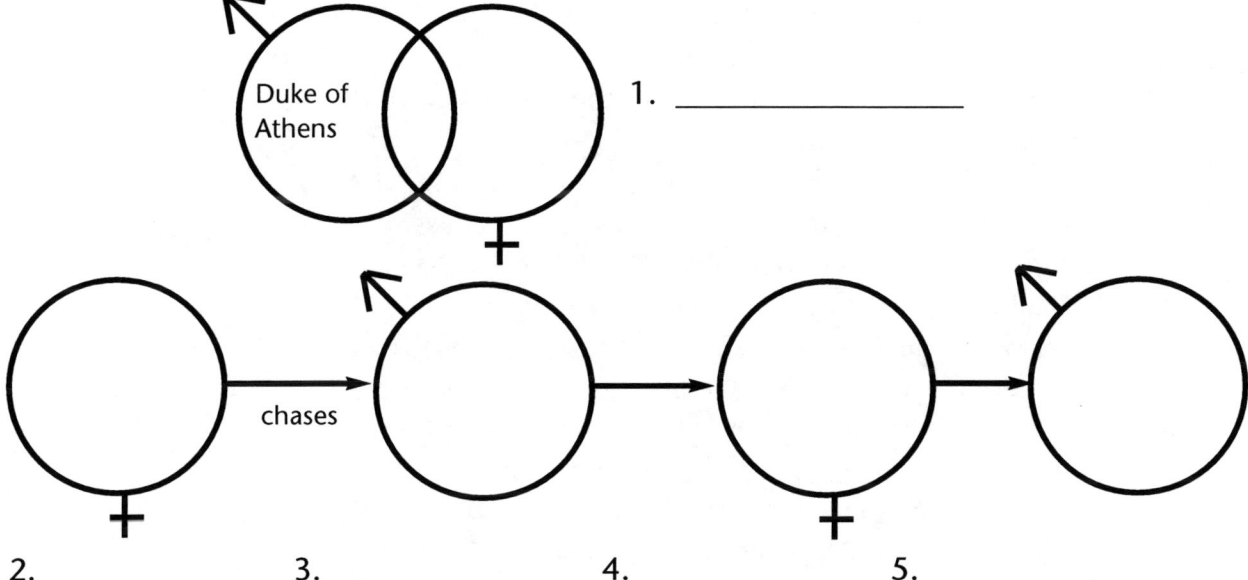

1. _____

2. _____ 3. _____ 4. _____ 5. _____

As you read the play, create some new graphics of your own to show other character relationships. When you finish the play, make some drawings that show the changes that have occurred in some of the relationships.

Directions: Read the quotes and think about how someone today might express the same idea. Place the letter of the correct paraphrase in the blank.

____ 1. "The course of true love never did run smooth." (Lysander, 1.1.134)
   a. Being in love is never easy.
   b. Be true to the one you love, or you will be sorry.

____ 2. "So quick bright things come to confusion." (Lysander, 1.1.149)
   a. Don't be blinded by insincere compliments.
   b. Good things often don't last long.

____ 3. "Love looks not with the eyes, but with the mind." (Helena, 1.1.234)
   a. When you're in love, you don't see your lover's flaws.
   b. When you're in love, you forget your troubles.

____ 4. "Ill met by moonlight, proud Titania." (Oberon, 2.1.60)
   a. You don't look so well by moonlight, Titania.
   b. It would be better if we hadn't run into each other here, Titania.

____ 5. "I'll put a girdle round about the earth
In forty minutes." (Puck, 2.1.175-176)
   a. I'll go around the globe in a jiffy.
   b. I'll blow down a strip of trees that goes around the earth.

____ 6. "My Oberon! What visions have I seen!
Methought I was enamored of an ass." (Titania, 4.1.75-76)
   a. Oberon! I dreamed I was in love with an ass.
   b. Oberon! Finally I realize what a jerk I was to love you!

____ 7. "The lunatic, the lover, and the poet
Are of imagination all compact." (Theseus, 5.1.7-8)
   a. Lunatics and poets have little imagination, compared with lovers.
   b. Crazies, lovers, and poets all have big imaginations.

____ 8. "For Oberon is passing fell and wrath
Because that she as her attendant hath
A lovely boy, stolen from an Indian king." (Puck, 2.1.20-22)
   a. Oberon is angry that she tripped him in order to steal the boy.
   b. Oberon is very angry that she stole a boy and made him her servant.

____ 9. "Look when I vow, I weep; and vows so born
In their nativity all truth appears" (Lysander, 3.2.124-125)
   a. Can't you tell by my tears that I mean what I say?
   b. Don't be fooled by crocodile tears.

Name_____

Shakespeare used many words which we use today—but in an UNFAMILIAR way. For example, when Quince tells Flute,"*You shall play it in a mask, and you may speak as small as you will,*" he means "You may speak it in as high-pitched a voice as you like" (NOT...you may speak it in a whispery "small" voice).

Directions: Circle the definition which BEST fits the underlined word in the sentences below. If Shakespeare uses the word as it is commonly used today, circle choice (d).

1. "Demetrius, I'll avouch it to his <u>head,</u>
   Made love to Nedar's daughter, Helena" (Lysander, 1.1. 106-107)
   a) protector   b) face   c) king   d) head

2. "Let me play the <u>lion</u> too." (Bottom, 1.2. 64)
   a) main role   b) lover   c) donkey   d) lion

3. "The human mortals <u>want</u> their winter here." (Titania, 2.1. 101)
   a) lack   b) dislike   c) have   d) want

4. "The dove pursues the griffin, the mild hind
   Makes speed to catch the tiger—<u>bootless</u> speed..." (Helena, 2.1. 232-233)
   a) slow   b) great   c) fruitless   d) bootless

5. "...Athenian found I none
   On whose eyes I might <u>approve</u>
   This flower's force in stirring love." (Puck, 2.2. 72-74)
   a) press   b) increase   c) test   d) approve

6. "...I will walk up and down here, and will <u>sing</u>..." (Bottom, 3.1. 117-118)
   a) whistle   b) shout   c) speak   d) sing

7. "How now mad spirit? What night rule now about this <u>haunted</u> grove?" (Oberon, 3.2. 4-5)
   a) seldom visited b) shadowy   c) much frequented d) haunted

8. "And Helena of Athens <u>look</u> thou find." (Oberon, 3.2. 95)
   a) be sure   b) try   c) in the east   d) look

9. "May all to Athens back again <u>repair</u>." (Oberon, 4.1. 66)
   a) repeat   b) return   c) repent   d) repair

10. "Now will I to the chink,
    To spy <u>an</u> I can hear my Thisbe's face." (Pyramus, 5.1. 191-192)
    a) if   b) so   c) when   d) an

17

Directions: Shakespeare used certain words that were familiar to his listeners, but sound archaic and old-fashioned to us. Match the archaic terms on the left with their present-day "translations." Then include each archaic term in a sentence of your own, on the back of this paper. Try to sound as "Shakespearean" as you can!

___	1.	belike	a.	speck
___	2.	air	b.	mirror
___	3.	glass	c.	at once
___	4.	waggish	d.	music
___	5.	eyne	e.	very likely
___	6.	marry	f.	also
___	7.	con	g.	read
___	8.	anon	h.	increase
___	9.	perforce	i.	usual
___	10.	waxen	j.	just now
___	11.	wanton	k.	playful
___	12.	wonted	l.	(a mild oath)
___	13.	wode	m.	handsome
___	14.	leave	n.	eyes
___	15.	o'erlook	o.	learn by heart
___	16.	toward	p.	mad
___	17.	eke	q.	forcibly
___	18.	fair	r.	give up
___	19.	mote	s.	about to take place
___	20.	erewhile	t.	luxuriant
___	21.	for aye	u.	cowardly wretch
___	22.	recreant	v.	breast
___	23.	aby	w	intellect
___	24.	wit	x.	pay for
___	25.	pap	y.	forever

Directions: You are Helena. You decide to write to a newspaper columnist for advice. Finish the letter you started, below:

Dear Gabby,

I have read your column for years, but I never thought that I would be writing to you. I've tried going to meetings of "Women who love too much" but I'm still hurting, so I thought maybe you could help me. My problem is that the guy I love doesn't want to be in the same room with me...

_____

_____

_____

_____

_____

In small group, brainstorm possible actions Helena might take and weigh the pros and cons of each. (A chart for organizing your ideas is shown below.) Then write a letter of advice to Helena, using details from the completed chart.

Choice #1		Choice #2		Choice #3	
Description:		Description:		Description:	
Pros	Cons	Pros	Cons	Pros	Cons

In literature, a **foil** is a person that through strong contrast underscores or enhances the distinctive characteristics of another. Write an essay supporting the thesis that Helena is a foil for Hermia. As a prewriting exercise, complete the Venn diagram below by filling in the blanks with words or phrases that describe each character. Characteristics that are shared by both characters should be placed in the overlapping area.

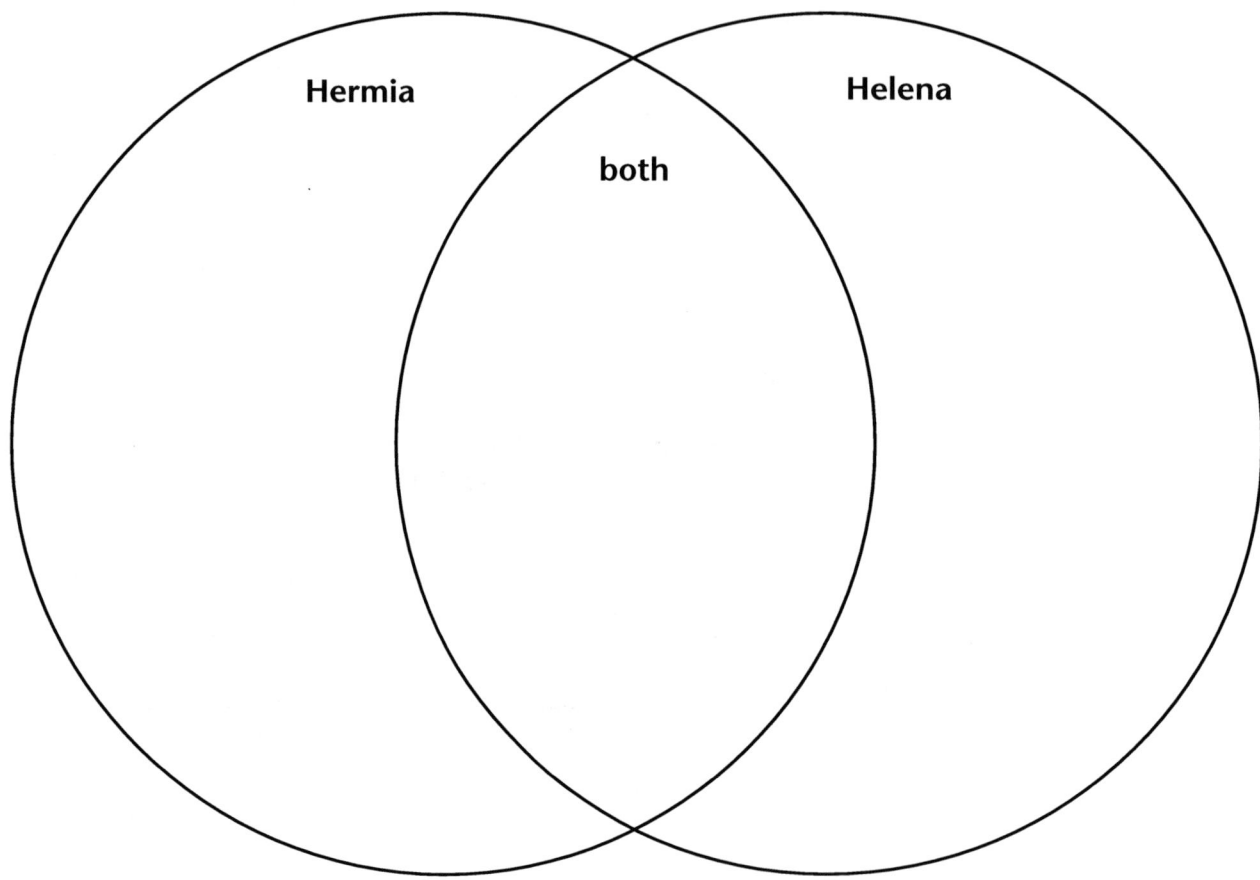

Hermia   both   Helena

Use some of the following transition words to help develop your ideas: *alike, also, both, common, equally, in the same way, just as/so, likewise, same, too, similar, similarly, although, but, differ, different, however, in contrast, on the other hand, unlike, whereas, while.*

I. A **malapropism** is the mistaken substitution of one word for another word that sounds similar. Bottom generated several malapropisms, as did other characters occasionally.

> *Example:* "...but I will **aggravate** (malapropism for **moderate**) my voice so that I will roar as gently as any sucking dove"

1. Provide the word Bottom or Quince **meant** when he mistakenly substituted each word in italics.

    a. (Bottom 1.2.2) "You were best to call them *generally* _____, man by man, according to the *scrip* _____."
    b. (Bottom 3.1.34-37) "Nay, you must name his name and half his face must be seen through the lion's neck, and he himself must speak through, saying thus, or the same *defect*_____":...
    c. (Quince 3.1.55-56) "...or else one must come in with a bush of thorns and a lantern and say he comes to *disfigure*_____...the person of Moonshine"

2. List one additional malapropism (cite the word or phrase act, scene, and line).

    _____

3. Brainstorm a list of six pairs of words that sound alike.

    _____ _____   _____ _____

    _____ _____   _____ _____

    _____ _____   _____ _____

4. Use one of the pairs to write a malapropism that might have come from Bottom's mouth while he was enacting Pyramus, or talking with Titania and the fairies.

5. List characters from TV, literature, etc. who are known for their malapropisms:

    _____

II. A **pun** is an intentional play on words based on the similarity of sound between two words with different meanings.
   Example: They went and **told** the sexton and the sexton **tolled** the bell.

For each pun, below, identify the speaker and explain the underlined word's two meanings.

1. "Thou hast by moonlight at her window sung
    With <u>feigning</u> voice verses of <u>feigning</u> love." (1.1.30-31)

    Speaker:_____ a)_____ b)_____

2. "...your kindred hath made my eyes <u>water</u> ere now." (3.1.189-190)

    Speaker:_____ a)_____ b)_____

3. "There is no following her in this fierce vein./ Here therefore for a while I will remain./ So sorrow's <u>heaviness</u> doth <u>heavier</u> grow..." (3.2.81-84)

    Speaker:_____ a)_____ b)_____

4. Cite one additional pun:

    _____

5. Brainstorm a list of six homophones (words with different meanings that sound alike)

    _____ _____   _____ _____

    _____ _____   _____ _____

    _____ _____   _____ _____

6. Use one of the pairs to write a pun that might have been spoken by any character.

    _____

When a person asks a **rhetorical question**, a reply is often not required or even expected. The answer is often obvious and the question is often asked for effect—or to express incredulity. Look at Act 3, scene 2, lines 122-344. Below are four questions asked in this scene.

    1.   Provide the answers they elicit.

        a. Hermia: "But why unkindly didst thou leave me so?"

_____

        b. Hermia: "What love could press Lysander from my side?"

_____

        c. Lysander: "Why seek'st thou me? Could not this make thee know, The hate I bear thee made me leave thee so?"

_____

        d. Hermia: (to Helena) "What have you come by night/And stol'n my love's heart from him? "

_____

    2.   Which of these would you label "rhetorical questions"? _____

    3.   Which of these examples shows two people who are not really "hearing" each other? _____

    4.   Why aren't Hermia and Helena able to communicate very well?_____

_____

    5.   Why aren't Hermia and Lysander able to communicate very well?_____

_____

Cinquain

A **cinquain** is a type of poem that has five lines, each with a set number of syllables (2,4,6,8,2). Adelaide Crapsey invented the cinquain early in the 20th century. Often the focus is on a single vivid natural image that produces thoughts of something else (e.g., a rain cloud=unkept promises). The rhythm tends to be iambic (a stressed syllable followed by an unstressed one). For example:

In XAnaDU did KUbla KHAN
A STATEly PLEAsure DOME deCREE...

1.   Select your topic from the following list, or make up your own:
    •   the woods/Helena's memories of Demetrius' unkept promises
    •   moonlight/Titania and Oberon's animosity
    •   the bank where thyme grows/Oberon's feelings for Titania
    •   the bank where Hermia and Lysander lie/their feelings for each other

2.   Draft a cinquain.

_____ 2 syllables

_____ 4 syllables

_____ 6 syllables

_____ 8 syllables

_____ 2 syllables

3.   Read the poem to a partner and rework it to achieve an iambic rhythm.

Name_____

Pantoum

A **pantoum** is a 16-line poem that comes from Malaysia, originating before the 1400s. In the pantoum, there are eight original lines and eight new ones.

1. Select a character from the play and entitle your poem, For _____ (e.g., "For Shakespeare's Helena.")

2. Draft a pantoum.

Line 1_____ (also Line 13)
Line 2_____ (also Line 5)
Line 3_____ (also Line 16)
Line 4_____ (also Line 7)

Line 5_____
Line 6_____ (also Line 9)
Line 7_____
Line 8_____ (also Line 11)

Line 9_____
Line 10_____ (also Line 14)
Line 11_____
Line 12 _____ (also Line 15)

Line 13 _____
Line 14 _____
Line 15 _____
Line 16 _____

3. Read the poem to a partner and rework it so it has some rhyme (at the ends of lines or even within nearby words).

Diamente

A **diamente** is a diamond-shaped poem that often describes a transformation. There are many transformations in *A Midsummer Night's Dream:* Bottom's head changes into that of an ass, Lysander's love for Hermia changes course, Demetrius goes from despising Helena to adoring her, etc.

Draft a diamente about one of these transformations, or another that you identify from the play.

1._____

2._____   _____

3._____   _____   _____

4._____   _____   _____   _____

5._____   _____   _____

6._____   _____

7._____

Line:
1. one word-subject noun
2. two words-adjectives
3. three words - participles
4. four words-nouns related to subject
5. three words-participles
6. two words-adjectives
7. one word-noun, opposite of the subject

Name_____

True/False: Mark the true statements with a "T" and the false statements with an "F."

___ 1.   Theseus was a Norse king.

___ 2.   The play takes place during an ancient, mythical time.

___ 3.   Theseus conquered the Queen of the Amazons.

___ 4.   Theseus will soon marry Hippolyta, queen of the Amazons.

___ 5.   Egeus wants his daughter, Helena, to marry Demetrius.

___ 6.   Hermia loves Lysander.

___ 7.   Theseus rules that Egeus' daughter must marry Demetrius, become a nun, or die.

___ 8.   Theseus once wooed Helena.

___ 9.   Helena loves Demetrius.

___ 10.   Helena and Demetrius decide to elope.

___ 11.   A group of laborers is preparing a play to entertain Theseus and Hippolyta before their wedding.

___ 12.   The players have chosen a play about a handsome prince who saves a princess from a lion.

___ 13.   The players plan to practice "Pyramus and Thisbe" in the woods the next night.

___ 14.   Bottom is a loud, boastful joiner who is disliked by the other laborers in the play.

___ 15.   Quince, a carpenter, is the play's director.

Name_____

Directions: Below is a summary of the first act. Fill in each blank with the correct word, phrase, or name.

   The curtains open on the royal court of Theseus, the ruler of 1._____. In four days, proclaims Theseus, he will marry 2._____, Queen of the 3._____—and he can hardly wait. In comes Egeus to complain to Theseus about his 4._____, Hermia, who insists on 5._____. Egeus is furious that she rejects the one he has chosen for her—6._____, a young man who once wooed 7._____ best friend, 8._____. Theseus passes judgement: If Hermia persists in choosing Lysander over her father's choice, she must either 9._____ or spend the rest of her life as a 10._____. She has to decide by 11._____. Given this ultimatum, Hermia and Lysander decide to meet in the woods the next night, then 12._____. After promising to help the lovers, 13._____ turns around and betrays their plan to Demetrius, in hopes of winning his approval. Demetrius rushes off to stop the elopement, with 14._____ in hot pursuit. Meanwhile, a group of laborers is getting ready to perform a play at 15._____ wedding. Their play seems a rather inappropriate choice, since it details the death by 16._____ of two lovers, 17._____ and Thisbe. The director is 18._____, a carpenter, and Pyramus is to be played by 19._____, a loud, boastful 20._____. Quince arranges for the group to rehearse the following night in the 21._____—at the same spot where 22._____ and Lysander have planned their rendezvous.

Short Answer: Answer each question in one or two complete sentences.

   23.   Why are Oberon and Titania angry with each other?

   24.   What is special about the nectar of the pansy?

   25.   How does Oberon plan to help Helena win Demetrius back?

   26.   Who is Puck?

   27.   Why does Lysander tell Helena he loves her?

Name_____

Identification: Write the letter of the character's name next to the correct description.

____ 1.	He is in love with Hermia, but her father believes he feigns that love.	a. Theseus
____ 2.	She is in love with Lysander.	b. Hippolyta
____ 3.	He is a carpenter and the director of *Pyramus and Thisbe*.	c. Egeus d. Hermia
____ 4.	He is King of the Fairies.	e. Lysander
____ 5.	He is the suitor to Hermia preferred by her father.	f. Demetrius
____ 6.	She is the Queen of the Amazons.	g. Helena
____ 7.	This little practical joker is Oberon's jester.	h. Oberon
____ 8.	He is the fairy whom Bottom says he will call to stop bleeding.	i. Titania j. Puck
____ 9.	He is the Duke of Athens, betrothed to Hippolyta.	k. Peter Quince
____ 10.	She is a tall blonde woman in love with Demetrius.	l. Nick Bottom
____ 11.	He is the loud-mouthed weaver who plays Pyramus.	m. Cobweb
____ 12.	She is Queen of the Fairies.	
____ 13.	He is Hermia's domineering father.	

Sequence: Indicate the order in which the following events occurred in the play. Write the letters of the events in order next to the proper numbers.

____ 14.   (a) Titania falls in love with Bottom.

____ 15.   (b) The tradesmen run off into the woods.

____ 16.   (c) Demetrius loves Helena, as he once did.

____ 17.   (d) Oberon applies nectar to Titania's eyes.

____ 18.   (e) Puck turns Bottom's head into that of an ass.

Quote Matching: Whose words are these?

____ 19.   "The course of true love never did run smooth."
        (1) Lysander   (2) Hermia   (3) Helena   (4) Theseus

____ 20.   "So quick bright things come to confusion."
        (1) Lysander   (2) Hermia   (3) Helena   (4) Theseus

___ 21. "Love looks not with the eyes, but with the mind,
And therefore is winged Cupid painted blind."
(1) Hermia   (2) Hippolyta   (3) Helena   (4) Titania

___ 22. "Over hill, over dale,
Thorough bush, thorough brier,
Over park, over pale,
Thorough flood, thorough fire..."
(1) Puck   (2) Titania   (3) Oberon   (4) another Fairy

___ 23. "Ill met by moonlight, proud Titania."
(1) Puck   (2) Oberon   (3) Theseus   (4) Bottom

___ 24. "I know a bank where the wild thyme blows,
Where oxlips and the nodding violet grows,
Quite overcanopied with luscious woodbine,
With sweet muskroses and with eglantine."
(1) Puck   (2) Oberon   (3) Titania   (4) another Fairy

___ 25. "You spotted snakes with double tongue,
Thorny hedgehogs, be not seen;
Newts and blindworms, do no wrong,
Come not near our Fairy Queen."
(1) Puck   (2) Oberon   (3) Titania   (4) another Fairy

___ 26. "Lord, what fools these mortals be!"
(1) Puck   (2) Oberon   (3) Titania   (4) another Fairy

___ 27. "And though she be but little, she is fierce."
(1) Hermia   (2) Helena   (3) Puck   (4) Oberon

___ 28. "The lunatic, the lover, and the poet
Are of imagination all compact."
(1) Hippolyta   (2) Theseus   (3) Puck   (4) Lysander

___29.   "The iron tongue of midnight hath told twelve.
           Lover, to bed, 'tis almost fairy time."
           (1) Oberon   (2) Titania   (3) Puck   (4) Theseus

___30.   "If we shadows have offended,
           Think but this, and all is mended,
           That you have but slumbered here
           While these visions did appear"
           (1) Puck   (2) Oberon   (3) Titania   (4) another Fairy

Multiple Choice: Indicate the number of the BEST response

___31.   Bottom suggests that Quince write a Prologue explaining that the
           _____ is not real so that the ladies in the audience will not be
           frightened
           (1) lion   (2) suicide   (3) moonlight   (4) dagger

___32.   Bottom suggests that Snug should reassure the ladies in the audience
           about his role as _____.
           (1) lion   (2) Pyramus   (3) Thisbe   (4) wall

___33.   Snout's clothes are smeared with _____ to convey that he plays
           _____.
           (1) white paint, moonlight   (2) yellow paint, a lantern
           (3) sticky thorns, a thornbush   (4) plaster, a wall

___34.   During rehearsal, Quince yells that the place is haunted because
           (1) none of the players remembers his lines correctly
           (2) he sees four fairies fly by
           (3) he hears the voices Puck is producing
           (4) he sees an ass' head on Bottom

___35.   When Titania has the magic nectar in her eyes, she considers Bottom
           (1) foolish but handsome
           (2) odd-looking but funny
           (3) handsome and wise
           (4) odd-looking but wise

___ 36. When Titania tells her attendants to "tie up my lover's tongue," she
means
(1) Help him learn to bray.
(2) Help him get over being so tongue-tied.
(3) I love him and I want to cherish his every word.
(4) I love him but I do wish he'd shut up.

___ 37. If a community theatre group were putting on *The Miracle Worker* today,
Bottom would probably want to be
(1) Helen Keller
(2) Helen's brother, a minor character
(3) in charge of advertising
(4) all of the above

___ 38. Theseus probably would not be marrying Hippolyta if he had not
(1) been compelled to do so under Athenian law
(2) been put under a spell by Puck
(3) defeated her in battle
(4) let her keep an Indian servant boy

___ 39. Which of the following BEST describes Egeus?
(1) changeable as a chameleon
(2) laughing through his tears
(3) hard-headed but soft-hearted
(4) hard as nails

___ 40. If Egeus were a judge, which sentence would he be most likely to hand
down to his own son, the getaway driver in a robbery where a bank teller
was killed?
(1) community service
(2) ten years in prison, possible early parole
(3) life in prison
(4) execution

___ 41. Because of Puck's mistake
(1) Lysander falls in love with Helena
(2) Helena falls in love with Demetrius
(3) Demetrius falls in love with Hermia
(4) Titania falls in love with Bottom

___ 42. The audience is most likely to feel sorry for _____ when _____
(1) Egeus, he goes to see Theseus about Helena
(2) Demetrius, he tries to stop Helena from following him
(3) Helena, she responds to declarations of love by Lysander and Demetrius
(4) Puck, he reveals to Oberon that he has made a mistake

___ 43. If Hippolyta were alive today to choose a bumper sticker, which one would she probably prefer?
(1) Don't blame me. I didn't vote for Theseus.
(2) Do you know where your children are?
(3) Women's Rights NOW
(4) Stand by your man.

___ 44. If Demetrius turned out to be a wife-batterer, Helena would probably
(1) leave him after the first blow
(2) insist that Theseus punish him under Athenian law
(3) turn to Hippolyta for advice
(4) blame herself and take the abuse

___ 45. If you were invited to a birthday celebration for Puck, which present would he probably LEAST enjoy getting from you?
(1) a whoopie cushion
(2) a ticket for a ride on the Loop-de-Loop rollercoaster
(3) a leather-bound set of Shakespearean tragedies
(4) a pair of rollerblades

Essay

I. Analysis
Directions: Select A or B and write a paragraph with complete sentences and at least three clearly explained examples or reasons. Circle the letter of the question you answer.

A. How does the story develop the theme that "love is unpredictable"?

B. What are the four main plots of *A Midsummer Night's Dream*?

II. Critical/Creative Thinking
Directions: Select C, D, or E.

C. You are Helena. Demetrius, who once wooed you, now rejects you. Write an entry in your journal. List all the options you have, and jot down ideas about what you plan to do—and why.

D. You are Oberon. Write a letter of apology (or an apology poem) to Titania.

E. You are Titania. Suppose the first person that you see while bewitched is not Bottom, but Egeus. Write him a love letter (or poem).

Name_____

Identification: Fill in the blanks with the names of the characters described.

_____ 1. He is in love with Hermia, but her father believes he feigns that love.

_____ 2. She is in love with Lysander

_____ 3. He is a carpenter and the director of "Pyramus and Thisbe."

_____ 4. He is King of the Fairies.

_____ 5. He is the suitor to Hermia preferred by her father.

_____ 6. She is the Queen of the Amazons.

_____ 7. This little practical joker is Oberon's jester.

_____ 8. He is the fairy whom Bottom says he will call to stop bleeding.

_____ 9. He is the Duke of Athens, betrothed to Hippolyta.

_____ 10. She is a tall blonde woman in love with Demetrius.

_____ 11. He is the loud-mouthed weaver who plays Pyramus.

_____ 12. She is Queen of the Fairies.

_____ 13. He is Hermia's domineering father.

Quotations: For each quote, tell who is speaking to whom.

a. "To you your father should be as a god—
One that composed your beauties, yea, and one
To whom you are but as a form in wax"

11. said by _____ to _____

b. "Why art thou here/Come from the farthest step of India/ But that, forsooth, the bouncing Amazon, You buskined mistress and your warrior love/To Theseus must be wedded"

12. said by _____ to _____

35

c. "Believe me, king of shadows, I mistook.
Did you not tell me I should know the man/
By the Athenian garments he had on?"

13.　said by _____ to _____

d. "I never may believe /These antique fables nor these fairy toys./Lovers and madmen have such seething brains/Such shaping fantasies that apprehend/More than cool reason ever comprehends"

14.　said by _____ to _____

e. "Not Hermia but Helena I love/
Who will not change a raven for a dove?"

15.　said by _____ to _____

Short Answer: Explain in your own words what each of the above five quotes means.

16.　Quote a:

17.　Quote b:

18.　Quote c:

19.　Quote d:

20.　Quote e:

Answer each question in 1-3 sentences.

21. What changes does Bottom suggest in the play? Why?

22. What mischief does Puck have with Bottom and the other players?

23. What mistake does Puck make and how does Oberon reverse that mistake?

24. How does Helena react when two men declare their love for her?

25. How do Lysander and Demetrius decide to settle their dispute over Helena? Why do you think they didn't just ask which one she preferred?

26 How do Demetrius and Lysander end up sleeping in the same spot as Hermia and Helena?

27. How does Titania dote on Bottom and how does this make Oberon feel?

28. How does Theseus change the original wedding plans?

29. How do Theseus and Hippolyta feel about the strange story the two other couples tell?

30. How successful is the wedding entertainment, *Pyramus and Thisbe*?

Essay

I. **Analysis:** Select A, B, or C.

A. Explain how Theseus' actions set in motion and later resolve the problems of the other characters.

B. Write a character sketch of Puck. What is he like? What motivates him? What is his philosophy?

C. Trace the theme of the male conquest of the female as it is developed throughout the play.

II. **Critical** and **Creative** **Thinking:** Select C, D, or E.

C. In two or three paragraphs, write a persuasive essay in which you defend or refute Lysander's observation:
> *The course of true love never did run smooth.*

D. Consider the scene in which Lysander urges Demetrius to a duel over Helena. Explain how the situation would end if Oberon and Puck did not step in to correct Puck's error.

E. Several of the characters in the play seem to be having communication problems. Choose a scene where the characters aren't communicating very effectively—such as the argument between Oberon and Titania or the tension between Helena and the two men she thinks are mocking her. Pretend to be a psychologist. Make some suggestions about how the characters might open up communication.

Answer Key

Study Questions

Act I, Scene i

1. Theseus is Athens' famous and popular ruler. He is to marry Hippolyta on May Day. He tells Philostrate to find entertainments to help him pass the time before his wedding.
2. Egeus' daughter, Hermia, refuses to marry Demetrius. Egeus wants Theseus to pass judgement on his daughter.
3. Hermia is small, dark, spirited, in love with Lysander.
4. Theseus tells Hermia she can marry Demetrius, become a nun, or die. He is regretful, doesn't like having to pass judgement, and doesn't like the idea of lively Hermia's becoming a nun.
5. Hermia goes from being angry and frustrated to being overcome by love, when alone with Lysander. They agree to meet in the woods outside of Athens. They plan to elope by going to the house of Lysander's aunt, who lives outside of the bounds of Athens and Athenian law.
6. Hermia and Helena were best friends. Now Helena is jealous of Hermia because of Demetrius' attentions to Hermia.
7. Helena tells Demetrius about Hermia's plan to elope because Helena wants Demetrius' approval, wants to go with him even if it is only in pursuit of Hermia, his true love.
8. It is hard to know why Egeus prefers Demetrius; by Lysander's own account, he is as good a marital prospect as Demetrius.
9. We're going through the same frustration true lovers always go through. Let's learn to be patient.

Act I, Scene ii

1. The players are meeting at Quince's house to prepare a play to entertain Theseus and Hippolyta the evening before their marriage.
2. Nick Bottom is a weaver who will take part in the play. He tries to take over the meeting, wants all the roles.
3. Two lovers plan a secret meeting in the woods; thinking that the woman has been killed by a lion, the man commits suicide; finding her dead lover, the woman follows suit. This tragic story seems a strange choice for a wedding celebration.
4. Both are pairs of lovers whose parents do not approve of their relationship; both pairs plan to meet in the woods.
5. Bottom will play the lead, Pyramus.
6. Bottom—weaver—"bottom" is a weaving term for the reel on which thread is wound; Quince—carpenter—"quoins" are wedges; Snug—joiner—makes "snug" joints; Flute—bellows maker—a "flute" is a pipe on an organ; Snout—tinker—he probably fixes "spouts" of kettles; starveling—tailor—tailors were often portrayed as thin and "starving."
7. Snug will play the lion; all he has to do is roar.
8. The tradesmen plan to rehearse in the woods outside of Athens—the same spot where Lysander and Hermia have just agreed to meet.
9. Line 19: "What is Pyramus, a lover or tyrant?"

Act II, Scene i

1. Puck is also known as Robin Goodfellow.
2. Titania and her court will be arriving. Oberon and his attendants will soon be arriving too, and Oberon is still angry with Titania.
3. Titania stole a young boy in India and refuses to give the boy up to Oberon, who wants the boy to be his chief page.

---

4. Puck curdles milk, makes old women spill their cider. He enjoys mischief and likes to entertain Oberon, his master.

5. She believes that Oberon loves her. Oberon claims that Titania loves Theseus and has caused him to drop some of his mistresses.

6. Each blames the other; Oberon caused the storms, floods, plague, etc., to punish Titania for refusing to give up the boy.

7. Cupid's arrow missed a virgin and hit a pansy. Oberon plans to use the flower's nectar on Titania, to make a fool of her so that she will give up the boy.

8. Helena races after Demetrius, who tries to reason with her and even threatens her. Oberon feels sorry for Helena and vows to help her win Demetrius.

9. Your threats won't stop me. You threaten to hurt me in the woods, but you have already done your harm; you've made me act in a way that is a disgrace to womanhood. We're not supposed to give chase, as I do. I don't care if my pursuit ends in death by your hand—I love that hand that much!

Act II, Scene ii

1. Titania sends her fairies off to sing, cure the roses of disease, get batwings for coats, frighten off the owls.

2. The fairies are trying to protect her from animals such as newts and snakes.

3. He puts a curse over her so that she will fall in love with "some vile thing near" when she wakens.

4. Hermia does not think it is proper for them to be too close before marriage.

5. Puck presses the nectar on Lysander's eyelids because he thinks that Lysander is the Athenian Oberon described.

6. Lysander declares his love for Helena, who thinks he is making fun of her.

7. Hermia dreams that a snake has threatened her while Lysander sat smiling.

8. Hermia runs off to look for Lysander.

9. Helena doesn't see Hermia. Hermia, sleep and never come near me again. I'm sick of you. All I want is Helena.

Act III, Scene i

1. He is afraid that they will be frightened when they see Pyramus kill himself. He suggests that Quince add a prologue that explains that the suicide is not real.

2. He is afraid that the lion will frighten the ladies. Bottom proposes that Snug—the lion—reassure the audience that he is not really a lion.

3. Bottom proposes looking in an almanac to see whether the moon will provide the necessary moonshine the night of the show.

4. Quince decides to have Starveling carry a thornbush to indicate that Starveling is Moonshine; the man in the moon supposedly carried a thornbush.

5. Bottom suggests putting plaster on Snout's clothes and having him create a "chink" with his fingers, through which Pyramus and Thisbe can talk.

6. He turns Bottom's head into that of an ass, and when the actors run off, Puck chases them, using different voices.

7. He isn't bothered much, and struts around singing to prove it.

8. Titania falls in love with Bottom. She tells her four fairies to wait on him and take him to her bower.

9. When Bottom first meets Cobweb, he promises to come to him if he bleeds; people used to apply cobwebs to wounds to stop the bleeding.

Act III, Scene ii

1. Puck tells Oberon, who is delighted.
2. Oberon and Puck see Demetrius and Hermia together and Oberon realizes that he is not the lover he had intended for her.
3. She is afraid that he has been killed by Demetrius. She can't think of another reason why Lysander would have disappeared as she slept.
4. Oberon presses the nectar on Demetrius, so that he will once again love Helena.
5. Helena thinks that he is mocking her, now; this is too sudden a turn-about to be believable.
6. Helena is jealous of Hermia and thinks that her best friend has joined the men in making fun of her; Hermia thinks that Helena is making fun of her short height.
7. Lysander challenges Demetrius to a duel; both are in love with Helena and tangle as they try to protect her from Hermia.
8. Oberon tells Puck to lead Lysander and Demetrius around the woods, then press a potion on Lysander's eyes that will remove the spell so that all four lovers will think the episode may have been only a dream.
9. Puck tells Lysander: Sleep soundly as I apply the magic nectar to your eyes. When you wake up, you'll be in love with the right woman again.

Act IV, Scene i

1. She is putting flowers on his head, kissing his ears. The four sleeping lovers are nearby.
2. Bottom requests the crude triangle and bones for music, hay for food.
3. Oberon has talked Titania into giving the boy up.
4. He feels sorry for her when he sees her acting so foolishly over Bottom.
5. They are going up the mountain to watch a hunt. Theseus is surprised to see all four together, when there had been so much enmity a short time ago.
6. Egeus wants Theseus to pass judgement on Lysander for impeding the marriage between Demetrius and Helena. Instead, Theseus proclaims that there will be a triple wedding.
7. They have only a dim recollection.
8. Bottom plans to have Quince write a ballad about the "dream" Bottom had, a ballad that will fill out the play by providing Pyramus something to sing after Thisbe dies.
9. We'll hear more about how you came to be together, later. Egeus, I won't agree to do what you want—to bring the law down on Lysander's head. Instead, since the morning is pretty well shot, let's forget about hunting, go back to Athens, and hold a triple wedding feast.

Act IV, Scene ii

1. The tradesmen can't rehearse without Bottom. They believe that only he is up to the role of Pyramus.
2. There will be a triple wedding. They now feel at least three times as pressured and anxious about how they are going to perform without Bottom.
3. Bottom would probably have been rewarded by Theseus.
4. Bottom arrives and announces that their play has been selected for consideration by Theseus.
5. Bottom tells the others to check their costumes, practice their parts, give up onions and garlic.
6. Theseus is coming from the temple and now a double or triple wedding is planned. We would have had it made if we could have performed our play!

Act V, Scene i

1. The three pairs of lovers—Theseus and Hippolyta, Demetrius and Helena, Lysander and Hermia—are all married.
2. The Master of Revels tells Theseus that it is poorly acted by bumpkins, but the absurdity of such a situation appeals to Theseus.
3. Because he is nervous, he often stops midsentence and continues where he should halt—thus changing the meaning.
4. She is embarrassed for them, but later joins in the ridiculing.
5. He cannot see Thisbe through it.
6. He comes unraveled as Theseus and the others make fun of the play; tongue-tied, he simply explains that the thornbush is his thornbush, the dog is his dog, etc.
7. They laugh and make ironic comments.
8. Theseus can choose to see the epilogue or watch a dance; he chooses to see the dance.
9. Puck enters, then Oberon and Titania and their band of fairies. Oberon gives each fairy magic dew to bless the marriages of the three human couples.
10. Fly through the house dancing and singing this song.
11. Puck is sweeping, apologizing for the weak play, promising they'll do better next time.

Note: Answers for Activity #1 will vary; therefore there are no answers for this and other open-ended activities. In all such open-ended activities, students should justify their choices, providing reasons and examples in discussion with a partner or in a small group.

Activity #2: I. 1-livery; 2-collied; 3-condole; 4-changeling; 5-buskined; 6-leviathan; 7-brakes; 8-reremice; 9-troth; 10-darkling; **II.** 1-Theseus to Hermia; 2-Lysander to Hermia; 3-Bottom to Quince; 4-Puck to Fairy; 5-Titania to Oberon; 6-Oberon to Puck; 7-Demetrius to Helena; 8-Titania to Fairies; 9-Lysander to Hermia; 10-Helena to Demetrius; **III.** a-darkling; b-leviathan; c-buskined; d-livery; e-reremice; f-condole; g-changeling; h-troth; i-brakes; j-collied

Activity #3: I. 1-juvenal; 2-throstle; 3-gleek; 4-patches; 5-misprision; 6-engilds; 7-incorporate; 8-stealth; 9-welkin; 10-derision; **II.** 1-Flute to the audience of the play; 2-Bottom blustering aloud; 3-Bottom to Titania; 4-Puck to Oberon; 5-Oberon to Puck; 6-Lysander to Helena; 7-Helena to Hermia; 8-Helena to Hermia; 9-Oberon to Puck; 10-Oberon to Puck; **III.** a. misprision b. derision c. patches d. engilds e. stealth f. welkin g. juvenal h. gleek i. throstle j. incorporate

Activity #4: I. 1-gaud; 2-patched; 3-pumps; 4-masques; 5-hight; 6-moused; 7-imbrue; 8-brands; 9-prodigious; 10-mend. **II.** 1-Demetrius to Theseus; 2-Bottom to himself; 3-Bottom to the other player; 4-Theseus to the lovers; 5-Prologue to the audience of Pyramus and Thisbe; 6-Theseus, joking aloud about Snug; 7-Thisbe calling on his sword; 8-Puck to the fairies and the audience; 9-Oberon to the fairies; 10-Puck to audience; **III.** a-brands; b-hight; c-mend; d-prodigious; e-moused; f-masques; g-imbrued ; h-gaud; i-pumps; j-patched

Activity #5: 1. Hippolyta, Queen of the Amazons; 2. Helena; 3. Demetrius; 4. Hermia; 5. Lysander

Activity #6: 1. a; 2-b; 3-a; 4-b; 5-a; 6-a; 7-b; 8-b; 9-a

Activity #7: 1-b; 2-d; 3-a; 4-c; 5-c; 6-d; 7-a; 8-a; 9-b; 10-a

Activity #8: 1-e; 2-d; 3-b; 4-k; 5-n; 6-l; 7-o; 8-c; 9-q; 10-h; 11-t; 12-i; 13-p; 14-r; 15-g; 16-s; 17-f; 18-m; 19-a; 20-j; 21-y; 22-u; 23-x; 24-w; 25-v

Activity #9: Answers will vary.

Activity #10: Hermia and Helena are both "well-bred," beautiful, young Athenian women, formerly best of friends. Hermia is short, dark, and spirited while Helena is tall, fair, more calm.

Activity #11: **I.** 1. a-individual, script; b-effect; c-figure; 2-5 vary; **II.** Speaker: Egeus; a-counterfeiting; b-desirous; 2-Speaker: Bottom; a-weep; b-sting; 3-Demetrius; a-harder to bear; b-more drowsy; 4-6 vary

Activity #12: 1. a. Lysander answers with a question: "Why should he stay whom love doth press to go?" b. "Lysander's love that would not let him bide—" c. "You speak not as you think" d. Helena answers with a question: "Fine, i'faith! Have you no modesty, no maiden shame/ No taste of bashfulness? What, will you tear/ Impatient answers from my gentle tongue? 2. all of them 3. all of them 4. Hermia is too distraught by Lysander's turn-about to think clearly; Helena is too upset by what she perceives as Lysander's and Hermia's mockery to listen well. 5. Hermia is hurt by Lysander's behavior and Lysander is blinded by love for Helena; both are guided by passion, can neither think nor speak logically.

Activity #13: open-ended

Comprehension Quiz (Level 1)
1-F; 2-T; 3-T; 4-T; 5-T; 6-T; 7-T; 8-F; 9-T; 10-F; 11-T; 12-F; 13-T; 14-F; 15-T

Comprehension Quiz (Level 2)
1-Athens; 2-Hippolyta; 3-Amazons; 4-daughter; 5-declaring her love for Lysander; 6-Demetrius; 7-Hermia's; 8-Helena; 9-die; 10-virgin priestess (nun); 11-Theseus' wedding day; 12-elope; 13-Helena; 14-Helena; 15-Theseus and Hippolyta's; 16-suicide; 17-Pyramus; 18-Quince; 19-Bottom; 20-weaver; 21-woods; 22-Hermia. 23. Titania has a boy from India; Oberon wants the boy as his servant. 24. When applied to a person's eyes, that person falls in love with the next one he or she sees. 25. Oberon plans for Puck to press the magic nectar on Demetrius' eyes so that Demetrius will fall in love with Helena again. 26. Puck is a tiny imp, Oberon's jester. 27. Puck has accidentally pressed the magic nectar on Lysander's eyes, instead of Demetrius'.

<u>Unit</u> <u>Test</u> (Level 1)
Identification: 1-E; 2-D; 3-K; 4-H; 5-F; 6-B; 7-J; 8-M; 9-A; 10-G; 11-L; 12-I; 13-C
Sequence: 14-E; 15-B; 16-D; 17-A; 18-C
Quote Matching: 19-1; 20-1; 21-3; 22-4; 23-2; 24-2; 25-4; 26-1; 27-2; 28-2; 29-4; 30-1
Multiple Choice: 31-2; 32-1; 33-4; 34-4; 35-3; 36-4; 37-4; 38-3; 39-4; 40-4; 41-1; 42-3; 43-4; 44-4; 45-3
Essay: <u>I.</u> <u>A.</u> Students should mention that Demetrius woos Helena, then drops her; Hippolyta fights Theseus, then marries him; Lysander loves Hermia, but under the influence of the magic nectar, rejects her; Demetrius loves Hermia, but under the influence of the nectar, falls in love with Helena; a lovely fairy queen, Titania, falls in love with a ludicrous mortal, Bottom.
<u>B.</u> Students should mention the tradesmen and their play, Oberon's dispute with Titania, the four lovers in the wood, and Theseus' upcoming marriage to Hippolyta. <u>II.</u> <u>C.</u> Helena might consider forgetting Demetrius, finding someone else, punishing Demetrius, trying to win Demetrius back. She plans to pursue him. <u>D.</u> Oberon might apologize to Titania for making her act foolishly while in love with Bottom. <u>E.</u> The letter or poem should reflect Titania's attraction to stern, uncompromising Egeus.

<u>Unit</u> <u>Test</u> (Level 2)

Identification: 1-Lysander; 2-Hermia; 3-Quince; 4-Oberon; 5-Demetrius; 6-Hippolyta; 7-Puck; 8-Cobweb; 9-Theseus; 10-Helena; 11-Bottom; 12-Titania; 13-Egeus

Quotations: 11-Theseus to Helena; 12-Titania to Oberon; 13-Puck to Oberon; 14-Theseus to Hippolyta; 15-Lysander to Helena

Short Answer: 16. Obey your father; he made you. 17. I know why you're here, you cad; you're here because you're sweet on Hippolyta, who's getting married. 18. Believe me, it was a mistake. You're the one who told me I would know him when I saw him. 19. I don't believe in fairies and magic. All these strange stories the lovers are telling are due to lovesickness; love scrambles your brain. 20. I love Hermia now. Who wouldn't give up a woman who's dark-haired and aggressive for one who's gentle and lovely? 21. Bottom wants a Prologue to explain that the suicide isn't real and the "lion" to tell the audience he is only an actor, so that the women won't be frightened. 22. He turns Bottom's head into that of an ass and misleads the player, using different voices. 23. Puck puts the nectar into Lysander's eyes instead of Demetrius'; Oberon has Puck put an antidote on Lysander's eyes. 24. She thinks they are mocking her. 25. They decide to have a duel. They seem to subscribe to the same Athenian male-dominated code of love that Egeus does. 26. Puck taunts each man with the voice of the other so that they rush around the wood until they are exhausted and happen to fall asleep near Hermia and Helena. 27. Oberon pities Titania when he finds her acting so foolishly—praising him with poetry, having her fairies wait on him, rubbing his hairy ears, etc. 28. He calls for a triple wedding. 29. Hippolyta wonders about the story, and thinks that something strange must have happened to bring the lovers all together, but ever-rational Theseus finds it unbelievable. 30. The acting is so awful that Theseus and the others find it hilarious.

I. Analysis

A. Students should trace the effect of Theseus' decision that Hermia cannot choose to marry Demetrius. Consequently she runs off to elope, which brings the other lovers into the wood, where their lives become entangled with the fairies' and the tradesmen's. At the end, it is Theseus' decision to have a triple wedding and to watch Pyramus and Thisbe that solves almost everyone's problems.

B. Puck is impish, a practical joker, loves to make Oberon laugh, and finds human behavior quite laughable.

C. Students might mention Theseus' conquest of Hippolyta, Queen of the Amazons; Lysander's and Demetrius' decision to duel it out over Helena, rather than consulting her; Oberon's "winning" the boy from Titania.

II. Critical and Creative Thinking

C. Students who choose this topic should include supportive evidence from their own life, reading, and/or observations.

D. Some students might envision one young man killing the other, and consequent suicides among the women—somewhat paralleling what happens in *Pyramus and Thisbe*; plucky Hermia might come along and stop the duel.

E. The psychologist might try to get Oberon and Titania to consider some compromise over the boy; Helena might be encouraged to examine some of the false assumptions she makes whenever she speaks to Demetrius or Helena: that she can't live without him, that Helena must be inviting Demetrius' attentions.
